STEINWAY & SONS

SIMPLY ELEGANT PIANO

VOLUME I

THE STEINWAY LIBRARY OF PIANO MUSIC

The Steinway Library of Piano Music is published by
Ekay Music Inc., Bedford Hills, New York 10507

Editor-in-chief: Edward Shanaphy
Project Coordinator: Stuart Isacoff
Designed by Luke Daigle/Daigle Interactive LLC
Production by Anita Tumminelli

Distributed by Warner Bros. Publications, Inc.
and Ekay Music Inc.

www.musicbooksnow.com

CONTENTS

A NOTE ABOUT 'LAY-FLAT' BINDING

This special binding is designed to keep your music book open on the music stand. It will need a slight preparation on your part to help it accomplish this. Place the book on a clean, flat surface and open it to a section near the front. With the heel of your hand, apply a gentle but firm pressure at various spots along the spine where the pages meet. Do not strike at the spine, and do not run your hand or thumb along the spine. This could cause the pages to wrinkle. Repeat this pressing process at various places throughout the book to break it in. When you have selected a piece to play, repeat the process again for that piece, and you may also, at this point, fold the book back on itself gently squeezing the binding.

ABOUT THE ARRANGERS

PRESTON KEYS

A graduate of Brigham Young University, Preston Keys is a working musician whose arrangements for piano have been enjoyed by thousands of pianists. The best-selling book of pop standards, *Simply Beautiful Piano*, features his arrangements exclusively. His contributions to other piano books such as *Piano Stylings Of The Great Standards, Piano Stylings Of Classic Christmas Carols, Pop Piano Artistry* and *It's Easy To Be Great* are always enthusiastically received. A pianist of exquisite capabilities, he toured with the Buddy Rich Orchestra in the 1970s.

NOREEN LIENHARD

Noreen Lienhard is a contributing editor and arranger for both *Piano Today* magazine and *Sheet Music Magazine*. Her piano books, and books for which she has contributed piano renditions, include *It's Easy To Be Great, Professional Stylings For The Solo Pianist,* and *Keyboard Runs For The Pop & Jazz Stylist,* and are among the most sought-after on the market today. A remarkable pianist, she has performed with such jazz luminaries as drummer Joe Morello, saxophonist Pepper Adams, trumpeters Howard McGhee and Clark Terry, and she can be heard on bassist Rufus Reid's CD, *Back To Front*. Noreen has been featured on Marian McPartland's *Piano Jazz*, the National Public Radio show, and can be heard on the Christmas CD, *An NPR Jazz Christmas Vol. 2 — Marian McPartland And Friends*. She has taught music on both the college level and in the public schools.

STUART ISACOFF

Well known as a writer, editor, pianist and composer, Stuart Isacoff is editor of both *Piano Today* and *Sheet Music Magazine*, and author or arranger of numerous books and collections. A former student of jazz great Sir Roland Hanna, he performs piano recitals that combine classical works with jazz improvisation. Among his best-selling publications are, *The 20 Minute Chords & Harmony Workout* for Ekay Music, Inc., and *Temperament: The Idea That Solved Music's Greatest Riddle* for Alfred A. Knopf. He is the recipient of an ASCAP Deems Taylor Award.

THE
MUSIC

THE SHADOW OF YOUR SMILE

Words by Paul Francis Webster ~ Music by Johnny Mandell
Arranged by Noreen Lienhard

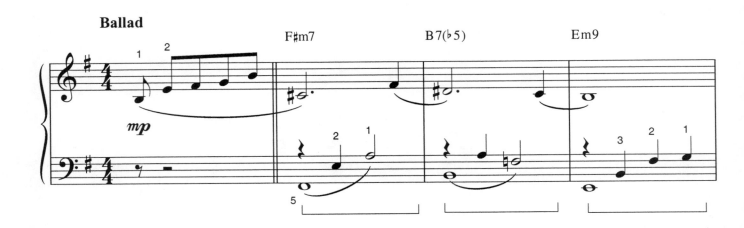

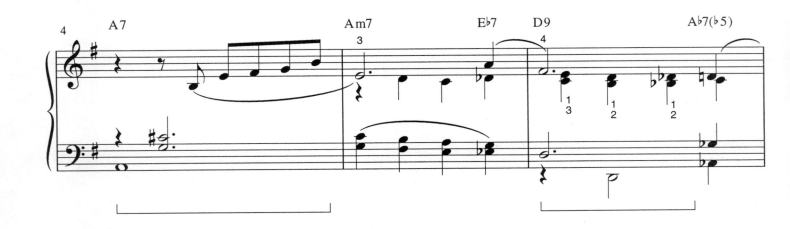

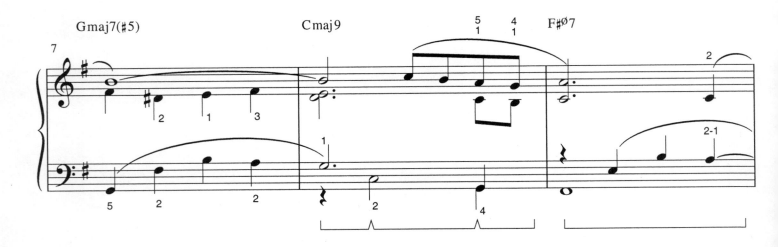

BEWITCHED

Words by Lorenz Hart ~ Music by Richard Rodgers
Arranged by Preston Keys

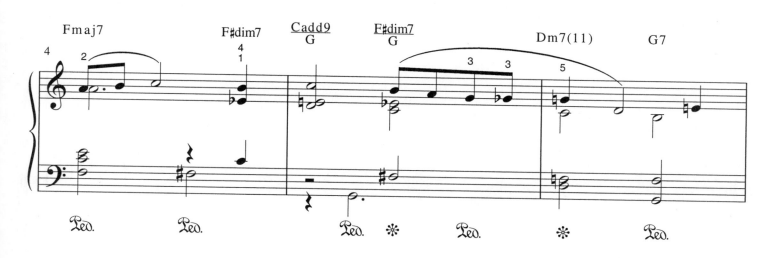

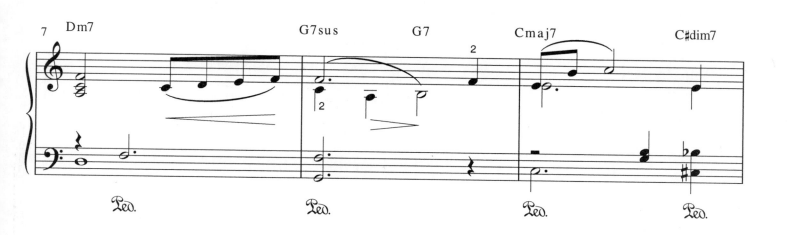

SHENANDOAH

Traditional ~ Arranged by Stuart Isacoff

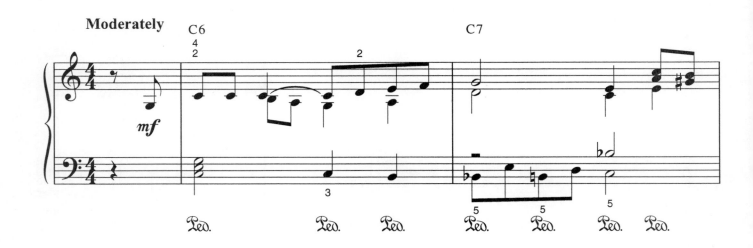

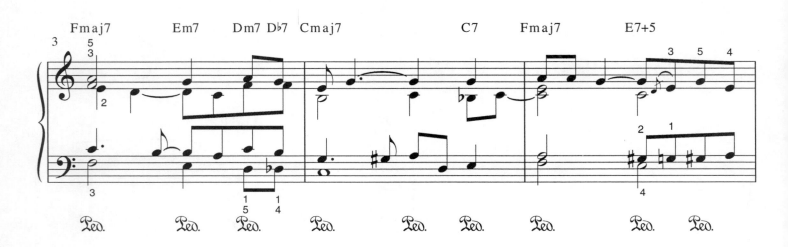

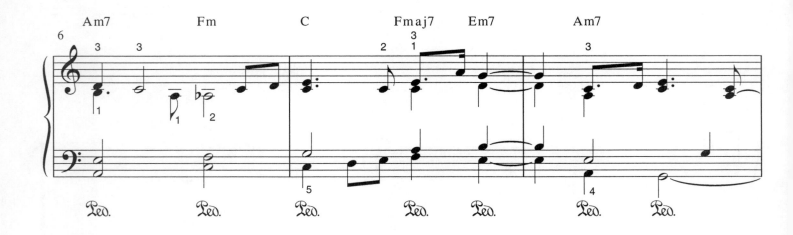

SOMEBODY LOVES ME

Words by B.G. Desylva and Ballard MacDonald ~ Music by George Gershwin
Arranged by Preston Keys

Moderately (In "2")

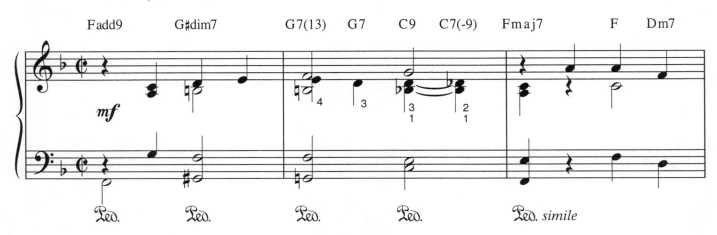

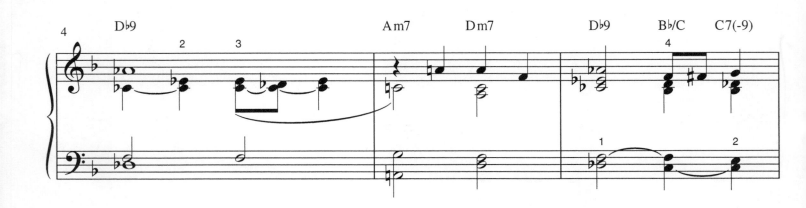

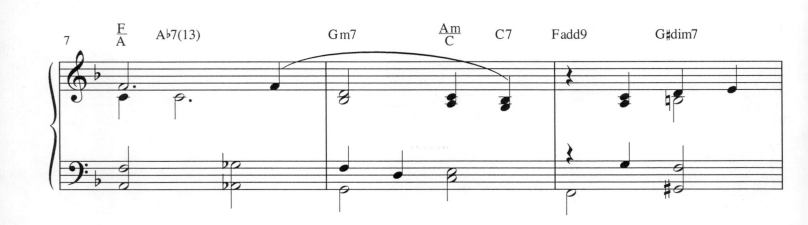

SWEET LORRAINE

Words by Mitchell Parish ~ Music by Cliff Burwell
Arranged by Preston Keys

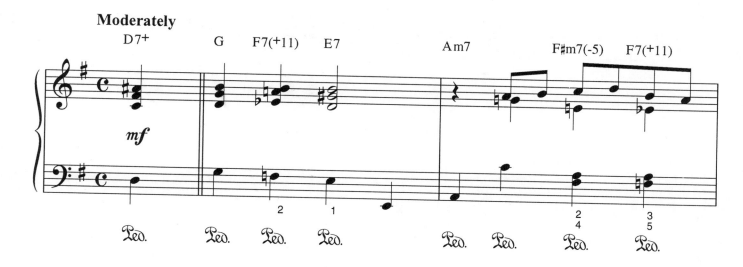

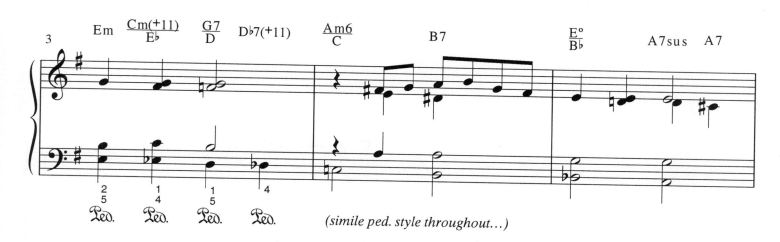

(simile ped. style throughout…)

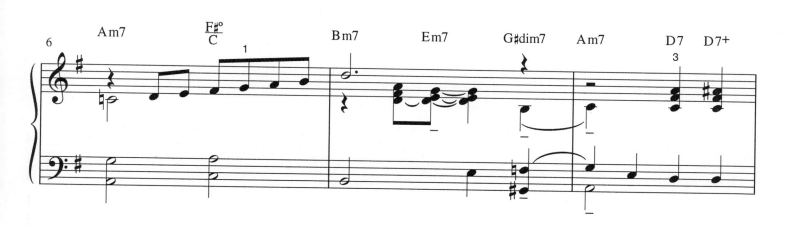

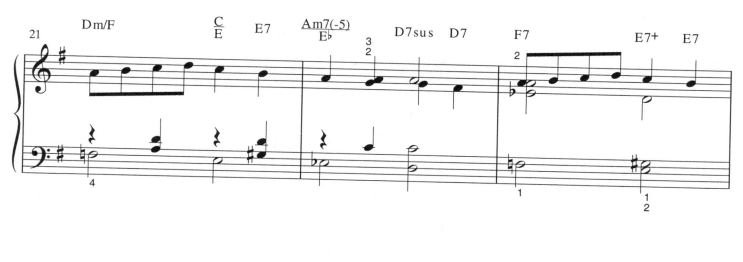

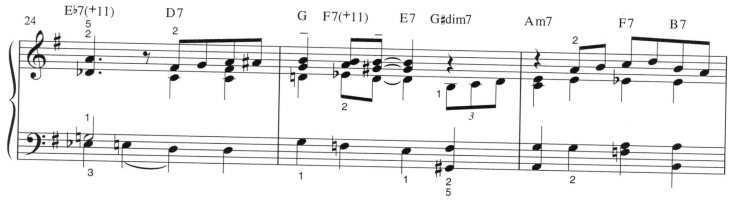

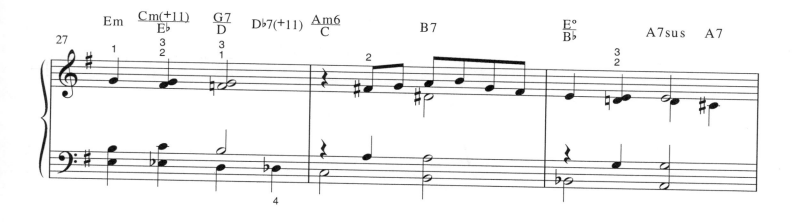

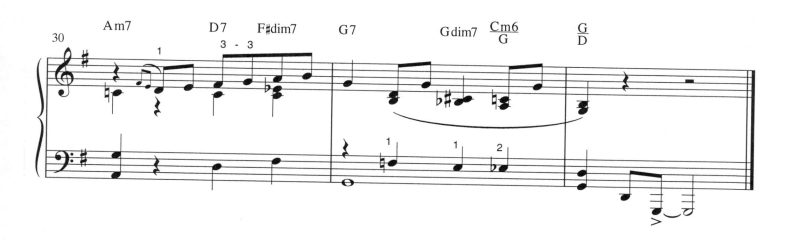

MEMORIES OF YOU

Words by Andy Razaf ~ Music by Eubie Blake
Arranged by Noreen Lienhard

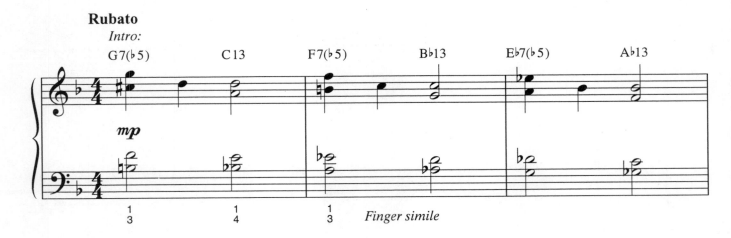

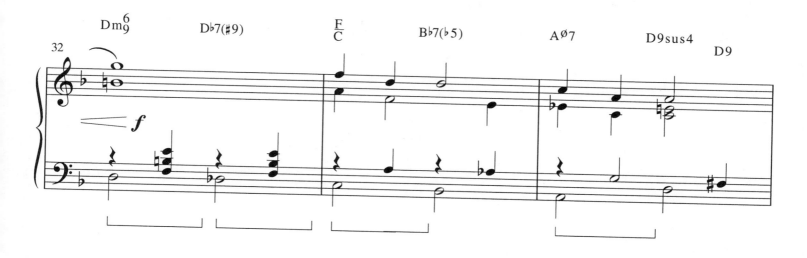

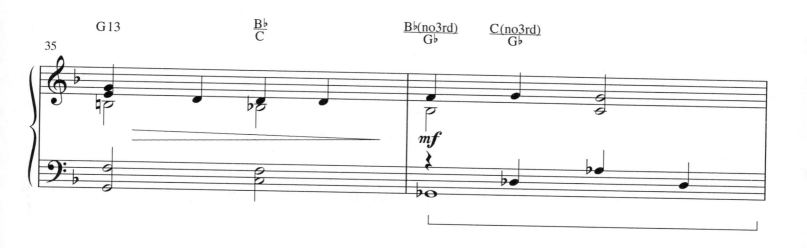

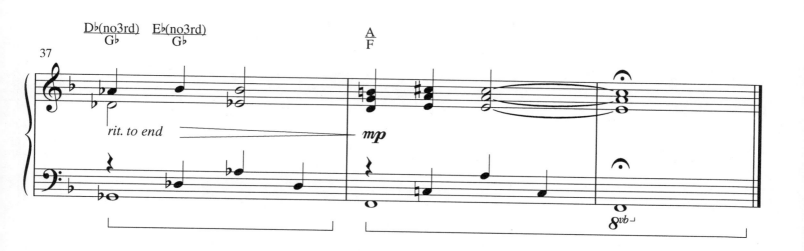

AT LAST

Words by Mack Gordon ~ Music by Harry Warren
Arranged by Noreen Lienhard

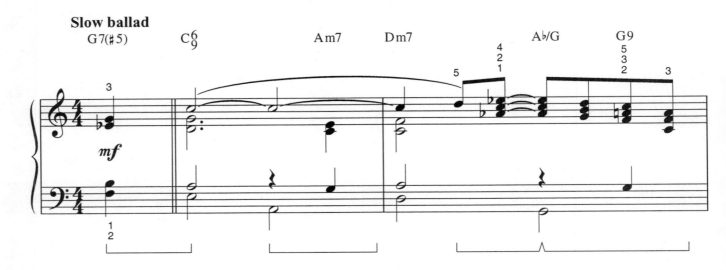

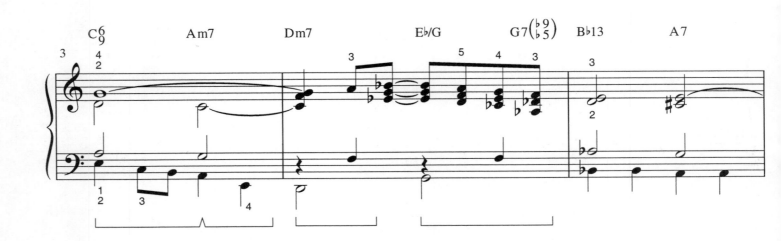

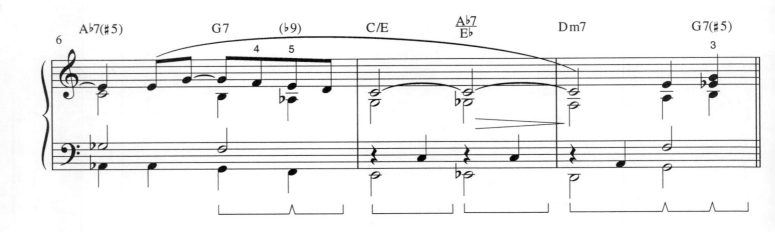

I CAN'T GET STARTED

Words by Ira Gershwin ~ Music by Vernon Duke
Arranged by Preston Keys

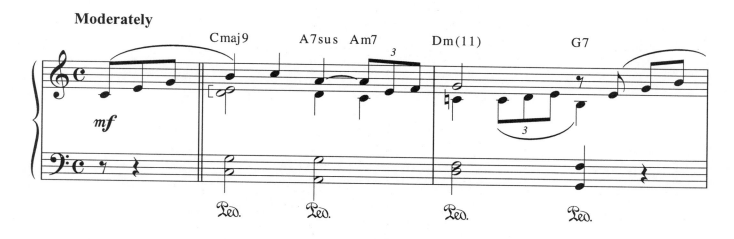

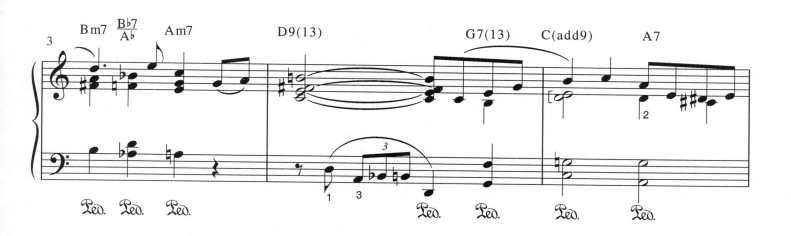

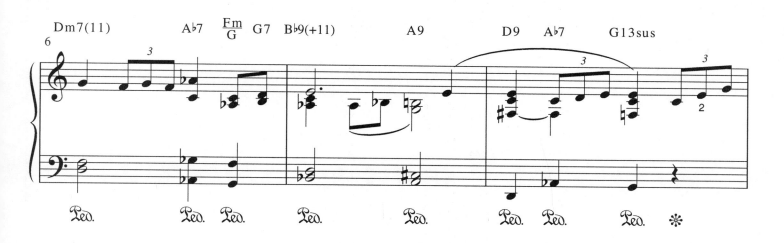

ON A CLEAR DAY
(You Can See Forever)

Words by Alan Jay Lerner ~ Music by Burton Lane
Arranged by Preston Keys

Moderately (In "2")

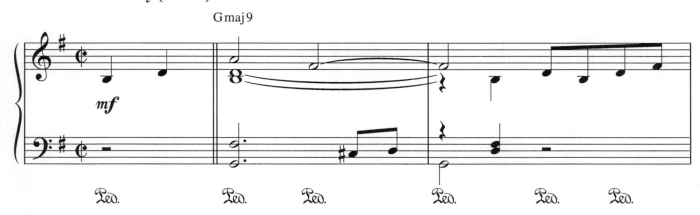

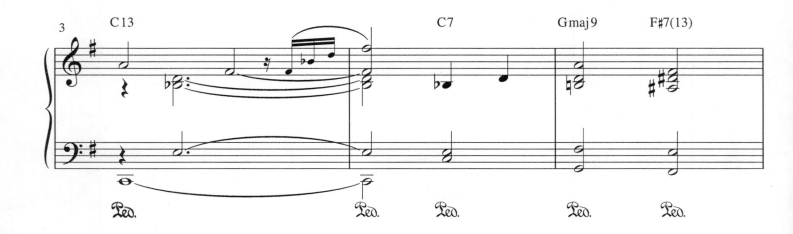

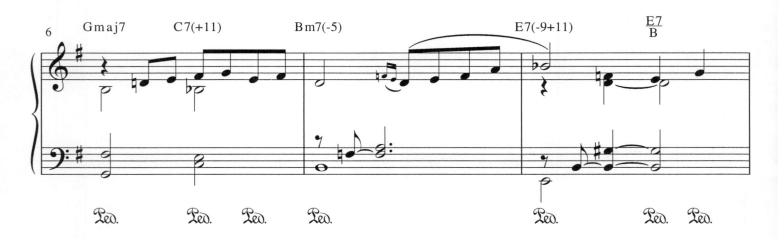

ON GREEN DOLPHIN STREET

Words by Ned Washington ~ Music by Bronislau Kaper
Arranged by Preston Keys

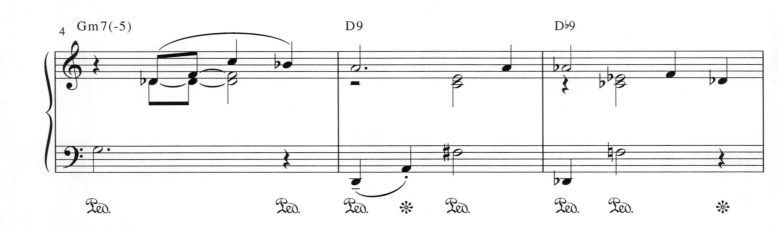

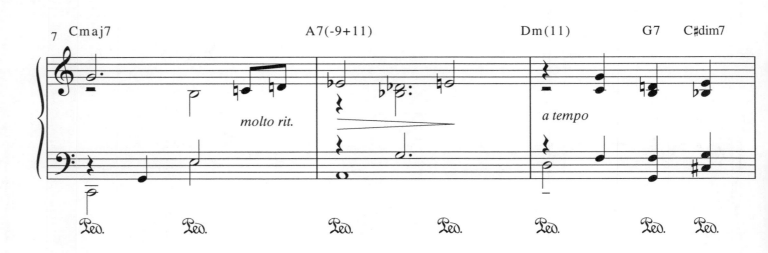

STAR DUST

Words by Mitchell Parish ~ Music by Hoagy Carmichael
Arranged by Preston Keys

MISTY

Words by Johnny Burke ~ Music by Erroll Garner
Arranged by Preston Keys

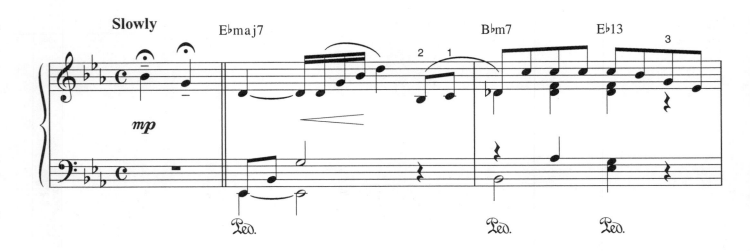

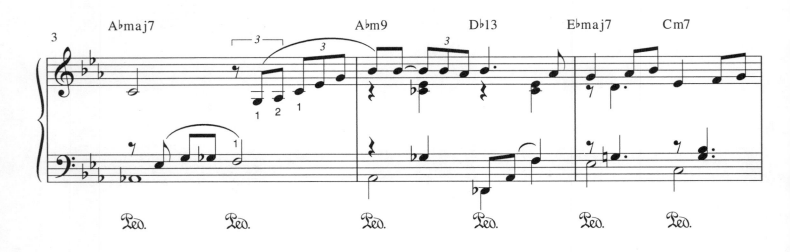

This lovely melody is a popularized version of Chopin's *Fantaisie impromptu.*

I'M ALWAYS CHASING RAINBOWS

Words by Joseph McCarthy ~ Music by Harry Carroll
Arranged by Noreen Lienhard

Medium
Intro:

Refrain

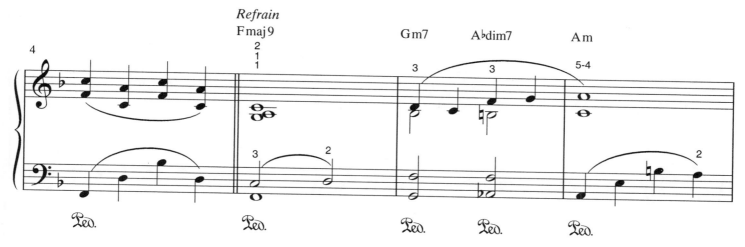

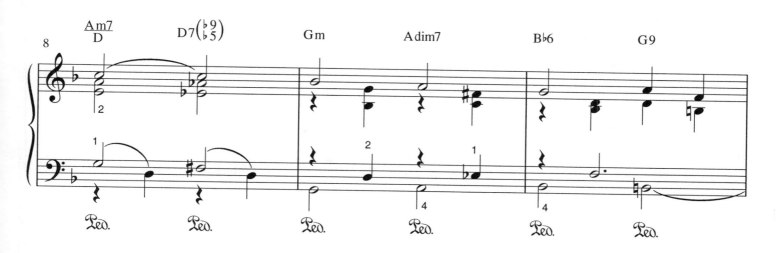

The great bossa-nova composer Antonio Carlos Jobim used Chopin's mournful *Prelude in E minor* as the basis of his song,
"How Insensitive." Here, Noreen Lienhard uses this same Chopin prelude to create a haunting, lyrical bossa-nova of her own.

HOW SENSITIVE

Music by Frederic Chopin
Arranged by Noreen Lienhard

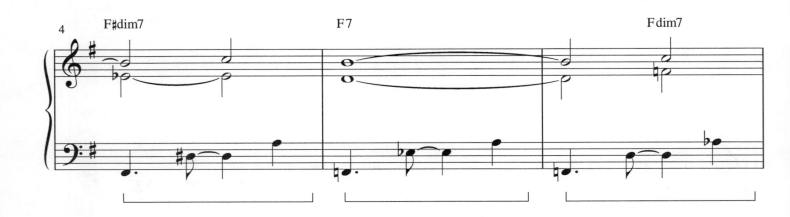

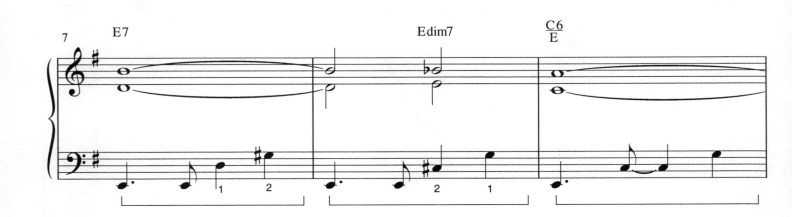

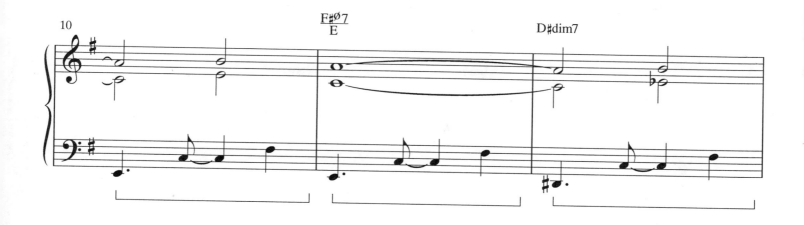

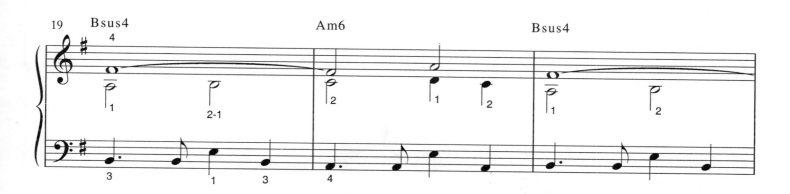

WHAT A WONDERFUL WORLD

Words and Music by George David Weiss and Bob Thiele
Arranged by Noreen Lienhard

Easy ballad tempo

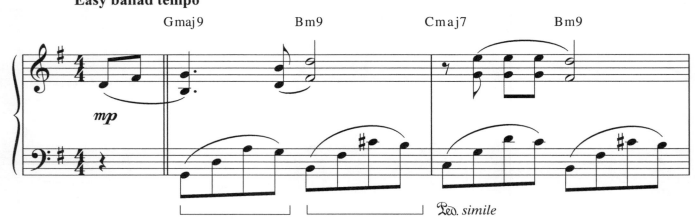

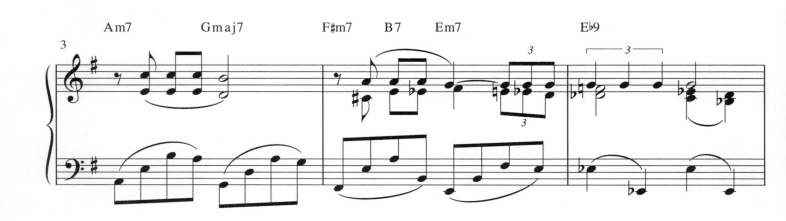

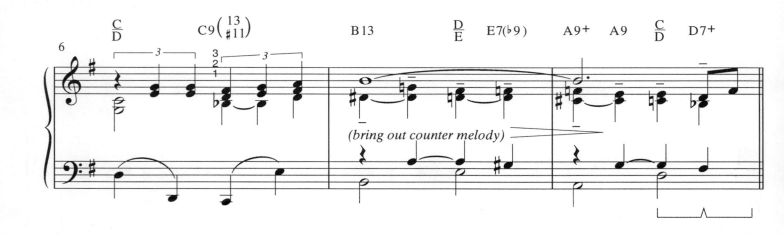

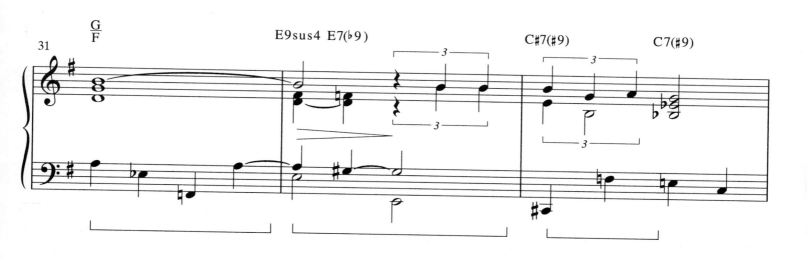

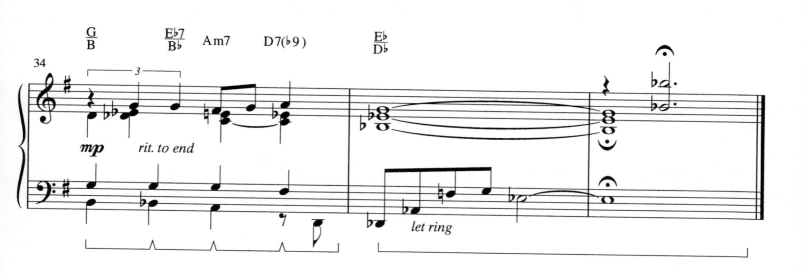